LETTERS FROM RUTH'S ATTIC

LETTERS *from* RUTH'S ATTIC

---

31 DAILY INSIGHTS *for* KNOWING GOD'S LOVE

RUTH BELL GRAHAM

Compiled from Decision *Magazine*

BILLY GRAHAM EVANGELISTIC ASSOCIATION

Charlotte, North Carolina

Scripture quotations marked NIV are taken from the Holy Bible, New International Version. ©1973, 1978, 1984 by International Bible Society. Used by permission of Zondervan Publishing House. All rights reserved.

Scripture quotations marked KJV are taken from the King James Version.

Scripture quotation marked RSV is taken from the Revised Standard Version. ©1946, 1952, 1971, 1973 by the Division of Christian Education of the National Council of the Churches of Christ in the United States of America. Used by permission. All rights reserved.

Scripture quotations marked NKJV are taken from the New King James Version. ©1982 by Thomas Nelson, Inc. Used by permission. All rights reserved.

These devotions include edited excerpts from *Legacy of a Pack Rat* and *It's My Turn* by Ruth Bell Graham and edited materials by Ruth Bell Graham previously published in *Decision* magazine. Used by permission.

ISBN: 978-1-59328-171-7

Foreword

My family and I have been deeply moved by the outpouring of condolences, love and prayers since my wife, Ruth, went home to Heaven recently.

I was glad when I heard that a little devotional book was being compiled from some of her short articles that have been printed in *Decision* magazine.

God gave Ruth many, many gifts, one of which was writing. Combining that creative writing ability with her practical nature, her sense of humor, an ability to see a good illustration, and especially her deep love for the Lord and knowledge of the Bible, she was gifted in putting down on paper little thoughts that God has used to inspire, challenge, and bless me.

I hope that these will be a real blessing to you, too.

Billy Graham
October 2007

Day 1

Let us throw off everything that hinders and the sin that so easily entangles, and let us run with perseverance the race marked out for us. —HEBREWS 12:1, NIV

Traveling Light

The Christian life is like climbing a mountain. For some people the climb is a gently sloping ascent; for other people the climb is like attacking the north face of the Eiger.

Christina Rossetti wrote:

"Does the road wind uphill all the way?

Yes, to the very end.

Will the day's journey take the whole long day?

From morn to night, my friend."*

Whether our climb is easy or difficult, we need to be in shape spiritually and to travel light.

To be in shape spiritually, we need spiritual nourishment and exercise. We need to spend less time reading about the Bible and spend more time studying the Bible. Then we need to apply what we learn—carefully and vigorously—to our lives, to live out daily what we have taken in.

To travel light, we need to lighten our loads. Some of us may need to trim off excess weight. Others of us have too many social involvements and too many meetings to attend. (Remember the caution: "Beware of the barrenness of a busy life.")

When the disciples were sent out two by two, they traveled light— "*without purse, bag or sandals*" (Luke 22:35, NIV).

Times change, situations vary, and God's orders to His followers are individualized. But the need and the message continue the same—and the goal. It's up to us to be in shape and to travel light.

———❧———

Prayer for the Day:

Father, please reveal the things that prevent me from fully obeying Your call. Thank You for guiding me as I drop these weights from my life.

*From "Uphill," by Christina Rossetti

Day 2

Be kind and compassionate to one another, forgiving each other, just as in Christ God forgave you. —EPHESIANS 4:32, NIV

Love Covers

My pet rabbit died abruptly (as pet rabbits have a way of doing). As a forlorn eight-year-old, in China, I buried him in our yard, lovingly digging a hole and covering him. Every day I dug him up to see how he was getting along. The last time I saw him he was green.

While I was growing up in China, someone in our greater mission family sinned, and I remember how quickly, quietly and effectively that situation was dealt with. Then the principle of "love covers" was applied. Not, like my pet rabbit, dug up again. And through the years in our own family, situations on occasion had to be faced, dealt with and buried.

Churches need to deal the same way, wisely and compassionately with sin, and then love covers: *"Ye ought rather to forgive him, and comfort him, lest perhaps such a one should be swallowed up with overmuch sorrow*" (2 Corinthians 2:7, KJV).

However, in those situations where some heresy, cult or con game operates under the name of Christianity, they need to be exposed so as to warn others. That is something different. But for those believers in God's family, sins need to be dealt with promptly, compassionately, privately. Then silence, under the principle of "love covers."

⁃

Prayer for the Day:

Father, teach me how to confront sin while still demonstrating Your grace and mercy to my brothers and sisters in Christ.

Day 3

Those who hope in the Lord will renew their strength. They will soar on wings like eagles; they will run and not grow weary, they will walk and not be faint. —ISAIAH 40:31, NIV

Ever Feel Like Running Away?

Sometimes it seems that troubles descend on us like a sudden storm that dumps 10 inches of rain in 24 hours. Troubles so often come in bunches or in such rapid succession that we barely have time to catch our breath between them.

We don't live on a perpetual high, and neither did the Psalmist David. He once longed for the wings of a dove so that he might fly away and be at rest (Psalm 55:6). We'd settle for the wings of a 747 plane—or even a Piper Cub!

In Isaiah 40:31 I discovered God's promise to us: those who *"wait upon the Lord shall renew their strength; they shall mount up with wings as eagles; they shall run, and not be weary; and they shall walk, and not faint"* (Isaiah 40:31, KJV).

So it boils down to running away or waiting. The key seems to be "waiting on the Lord" (cf. Isaiah 40:31).

In our "instant" generation most of us don't wait easily. But we need to learn. F.B. Meyer wrote, "Prayer means not always talking to Him, but waiting before Him till the dust settles and the stream runs clear."

Jeremiah, in the most dismal of circumstances, wrote: *The Lord is good unto them that wait for him*" (Lamentations 3:25, KJV).

———❦———

Prayer for the Day:

Today I will wait on You, Holy Spirit, and learn to listen for Your voice. I am grateful for the restoration You give when I linger in Your presence.

Day 4

*The apostles gathered around Jesus and reported to him all they had done and taught. Then, because so many people were coming and going that they did not even have a chance to eat, he said to them, "Come with me by yourselves to a quiet place and get some rest." —*MARK 6:30–31, NIV

When We Are Just Plain Tired

iscouragement is the devil's calling card, and he tries to discourage us by making us think that our frustration or irritability is a result of some spiritual fault. But we may be just plain tired.

Do you remember the Prophet Elijah? At one point he was so tired that he wanted to give up. He told God that he just couldn't go on. God didn't lecture Elijah on his faults and failures, causing him to be more discouraged than he was. No, God sent an angel to awaken Elijah and give him something to eat and drink. Then Elijah lay down and slept again.

When we are worn out or exhausted, or at the end of our physical

7

resources, Satan tries to persuade us that we have a spiritual problem. In reality our problem may be a physical one. And maybe, like Elijah, we need to get some rest.

———✦———

Prayer for the Day:

When I become tired and frustrated with myself, Father, please remind me to pay attention to the need for physical rest and nutrition. I know that in doing this I will be better equipped to do Your will.

Day 5

If you obey my commands, you will remain in my love, just as I have obeyed my Father's commands and remain in his love.
—JOHN 15:10, NIV

God's Greatest Pleasure

Tonight, as I sit on the porch, our old German shepherd is lying at my feet. As a low mutter of thunder rumbles in the distance, he lifts his great head and gives a deep warning bark. Then, as the storm nears, he rises with a lurch and tears into the front yard to meet it.

The storm is on us, the great dog furiously doing battle with it. As it passes, he returns to the porch, settling contentedly at my feet convinced he has driven it away.

Protecting and pleasing us is his very life.

He is a German guard dog, given to us years ago by concerned friends. He had been carefully trained in search and rescue, attack, and obedience.

I cannot imagine an occasion when we would give the order to attack. It's the obedience training that gives us real joy. To stop, to sit, to lie down, to go away, to search, to stay, to heel. A disobedient dog is not only a headache; he can be a liability. Obedience makes a dog a joy.

Is it less so with God and His children?

I think obedience, more than anything else, must give the Lord pleasure. Simple obedience. Joyful, eager, unquestioning obedience; to be able to say with the psalmist, *"I delight to do thy will, O my God"* (Psalm 40:8, KJV), would be the height of training for the Christian.

For it is this that gives God the greatest pleasure.

———✦———

Prayer for the Day:

Father, thank You for loving me enough to send Jesus to die for my sins. May I respond to Your great gift by obeying Your Word and abiding in Your love.

Day 6

The Lord is near to all who call on him, to all who call on him in truth. He fulfills the desires of those who fear him; he hears their cry and saves them. —PSALM 145:18–19, NIV

God Hears

The cat had kittens on the trundle bed in the downstairs guest room. We didn't think that was such a good idea, so we collected them and placed them on rags in a cardboard box in front of the kitchen fireplace until we could come up with something more suitable.

But the mother cat had a mind of her own. We watched with amusement as she entered the kitchen silently, stood on her back legs, front legs on the box, sniffing for her babies. Then leaping nimbly over the side, she checked them over, picked one up by the back of the neck, leaped out, and quietly returned it to the trundle bed. This was repeated until all that was left was the runt of the litter.

She did not come back. She may have been exhausted from her efforts, or she may have been busy playing lunch counter to the others. We waited.

Finally the tiny scrap in the bottom of the box let out more of a squeak than a mew. It was almost a non-sound.

Instantly, soundlessly, the mother cat appeared, bounded in and out of the box, the littlest kitten in her mouth, and carried it back to the guest room. Three doors, two rooms and two hallways away, and yet she heard. It wasn't even a full-fledged cry.

Nor are our prayers necessarily full-fledged prayers—or even articulated cries for help. According to the Bible, God responds to our sighs, our tears and our murmurs. Even our longings can be interpreted as prayer. John Trapp said in commenting on Psalm 145, "The Lord is near to all that call upon Him; yea, He can feel breath when no voice can be heard for faintness."

⟶

Prayer for the Day:

I am thankful, Lord, that You hear my faintest cries for help. Help me to understand how important it is to call out to You for help in every circumstance.

Day 7

The Lord said to Joshua, "Stand up! What are you doing down on your face? ... Go, consecrate the people."
—JOSHUA 7:10, 13, NIV

Do Something!

There are times, I have found, when praying is not enough. God says, as it were, "What are you praying for? Do something!"

Moses, hotly pursued by Pharaoh, cried out to God, who replied, *"Wherefore criest thou unto me? Speak unto the children of Israel, that they go forward"* (Exodus 14:15, KJV).

After Israel's ignominious defeat at Ai, the desperate Joshua prostrated himself in prayer before the Lord, only to hear Him say, *"Wherefore liest thou thus upon thy face? Israel hath sinned"* (Joshua 7:10–11, KJV).

If our hearts are listening as we pray, we will from time to time hear, "What are you praying for? Do something!" And we will know what it is we must do. There will be a wrong to put right, a sin to confess, a letter to write, a friend to visit or a child to be rocked and read to.

C.S. Lewis suggested that as we pray, Christ stands beside us changing us. "You may realize that," he wrote, "instead of saying your prayers, you ought to be downstairs writing a letter, or helping your wife wash-up. Well, go and do it." And again, "I am often, I believe, praying for others when I should be doing things for them. It's so much easier to pray for a bore than to go and see him."

And so it is with us. We must be quick to pray, and just as quick to obey.

Prayer for the Day:

Father, please open my eyes when I am stalling and refusing to do the things You have commanded. Grant me boldness to do the things I think are unpleasant or difficult.

Day 8

How to Start Praying

Men of God, whose prayers are recorded for us in the Bible, never read a book on prayer, never went to a seminar on prayer, never heard a sermon on prayer. They just prayed.

Satan fears prayer because God hears prayer. Satan will stop at nothing to distract a person from praying or to get him to postpone praying or, failing to do that, to discourage him in his praying.

This page is simply to encourage you to start.

Start praying where you are, as you are, about whatever concerns you, about whatever is lying most heavily on your heart, about whatever is irritating or frustrating you at present.

Suggestion: Keep a prayer list. Make your requests specific and date them. Then date the answer. Like the ungrateful lepers, we tend to forget. It may be impossible to date the answers to certain requests. For instance, if I pray for patience, I will not find that on such and such a date I suddenly become patient. But if I pray for guidance in a particular problem, for the conversion of a friend or for the resolving of some apparently hopeless difficulty, recording the answer as well as the request will be a cause for worship and a means of strengthening my faith.

Be pointed. Be persistent. Be patient. But pray.

Prayer for the Day:

Father God, I often forget to bring my needs and concerns to You and forget to thank You when You act in my behalf. Today I commit myself to prayer and to giving thanks when I recognize Your answers.

Day 9

Do not set your heart on what you will eat or drink; do not worry about it. ... Your Father knows that you need them. But seek his kingdom, and these things will be given to you as well. Do not be afraid, little flock, for your Father has been pleased to give you the kingdom. —LUKE 12:29–32, NIV

What Lies Ahead

ne day many years ago, as I was driving home from town with one of our sons, he kept urging me to hurry. "Go faster, Mother!" he insisted. But he was too young to read the road sign that said 45 mph. And again, "Pass him, Mother." But he was too small to see that there was a double yellow line.

Then I began applying the brake. "Why are you stopping?" he demanded.

"There's a school bus ahead that has stopped," I replied.

I thought to myself, "When God is at the wheel, we may request—but never insist. We are too young to read certain signs, too small to see what lies ahead."

George Macdonald writes, "There is a communion with God that asks for nothing, yet asks for everything. ... He who seeks the Father more than anything He can give, is likely to have what he asks, for he is not likely to ask amiss."

There may be a long interval between these two clauses from John 16:24: *"ask, and ye shall receive"* and *"that your joy may be full"* (KJV). But the end of true prayer is always joy.

———✦———

Prayer for the Day:

How good it is to know that I can rest in Your provision for me, Lord. When I am anxious and worried about the future, please help me to seek Your face instead.

Day 10

Live in peace with each other. And we urge you, brothers, warn those who are idle, encourage the timid, help the weak, be patient with everyone. —1 THESSALONIANS 5:13–14, NIV

The Sting of Life

I was swimming in the choppy Mediterranean Sea when suddenly my arm felt as if it had touched a high-voltage wire. Spinning around, I saw a tiny blue jellyfish swimming away. It seemed an eternity before I was able to make it the short distance back to the beach, petrified that I might be stung again. Before long, ugly welts rose on my forearm and back.

Later, as I compared notes with a friend who had suffered the same fate, he said to me, "I hope you won't let this keep you from going into the water."

I hadn't the heart to tell him I'd lost all taste for the sea.

But two painful days later, assured by other beach-bathers that the water was clear, I ventured another swim. My friend's familiar voice boomed, "Good for you! Keep it up!"

Long after the jellyfish attack, I remembered those words. Life is a lot like the sea: full of venomous creatures that attack without warning. I think of baby Christians who, after their first painful encounter, call it quits unless a stronger Christian offers a word of advice, a shout of encouragement.

Has anyone around you been stung lately?

———❧———

Prayer for the Day:

Lord, is there a new believer in Jesus who needs encouragement? Show me how to build them up and how to help them become an active member of the body of Christ.

Day 11

The Lord is exalted, for he dwells on high; he will fill Zion with justice and righteousness. He will be the sure foundation for your times, a rich store of salvation and wisdom and knowledge; the fear of the Lord is the key to this treasure.
—ISAIAH 33:5–6, NIV

Afraid of the Right Things

The shot through the rattlesnake's head had all but demolished it. The snake was twisting on the driveway, and the family gathered to look at it.

One grandson reached out to touch it. Bill grabbed him and held him back, explaining that even a dead snake can be deadly. Still, the boy was totally without fear and determined to grab the snake's tail. But as he reached for it, the snake's mangled head struck out. The boy jumped back, getting the message: Rattlesnakes are to be feared.

Education, it has been said, consists of being afraid of the right things.

We taught our children to be careful with matches and open flames; fear of house fires and forest fires prompts sensible precautions. We also taught them not to run into the street without looking both ways; a proper fear of cars is also legitimate.

There is one grand, noble fear we are taught from Genesis to Revelation—fear of the Lord. This is more than being scared. It is a reverential trust, not only a fear of offending, but a loving to the point that one would not want to offend.

Prayer for the Day:

Father, You have been so gracious to me. Keep me from taking Your mercy for granted and from ignoring Your commandments and Your presence in my life.

Day 12

I am coming soon. Hold on to what you have, so that no one will take your crown. Him who overcomes I will make a pillar in the temple of my God. ... And I will also write on him my new name. —REVELATION 3:11–12, NIV

Autographed by the Author

heavy, flat package arrived from Ottawa. Quickly tearing off the wrappings, I discovered with delight a portfolio by photographer Yousuf Karsh, complete with his comments on each subject and sitting. Wondering who had sent the book, I turned to the front and discovered an inscription to Bill from the photographer himself. The customs sticker on the torn wrappings described the value of the contents as "Autographed by the author."

I later re-read an essay I had written at age 14, titled "The Name of Jesus." It closes with Revelation 3:12: *"I will write upon him my new name"* (KJV).

The essay concluded: "If His present name is so wonderful, what will His new name be which He has promised to write upon us if we overcome in this world?"

Our ultimate value will not only be that we were created, compiled and, as it were, written by the Author—but that we have been autographed by the Author.

~⟶~

Prayer for the Day:

Thank you, Lord, for writing Your Name on me. Remind me that my ultimate value lies in belonging to You through faith in Your Son, Jesus Christ.

Day 13

A great persecution broke out against the church at Jerusalem, and all except the apostles were scattered throughout Judea and Samaria. ... Those who had been scattered preached the word wherever they went. —ACTS 8:1, 4, NIV

Barracuda!

We were out on a boat years ago when Bill and our son-in-law decided to go swimming. They lowered the ladder and started down. In his mid-sixties, Bill was still as trim as a 30-year-old, but he moved as slowly and stiffly as a 90-year-old.

"I'm getting old," he said as he looked carefully for the next rung. "It's harder to move all the time. I'm getting so stiff." Rung by difficult rung he slowly lowered himself into the water. Finally he and our son-in-law leisurely and blissfully swam.

My daughter Gigi and I were watching from the upper deck. Suddenly I saw a long, thin shadow moving swiftly through the clear, deep water toward the swimmers.

"Bill!" I shouted. "There's a barracuda!"

Zip! He was up that ladder in nothing flat, losing 50 years in a second!

God often uses sudden danger to move us. The handful of early believers were commissioned by Jesus to go into all the world and preach the Gospel. They met daily in the temple in Jerusalem to worship and praise God—until Stephen was stoned to death, and they were scattered. Persecution had begun. But so had the fulfillment of the Great Commission. By unexpected means God frequently makes possible the impossible by motivating the unmotivated.

―――――

Prayer for the Day:

Father, when trials make my life difficult, please enable me to see Your hand at work, motivating me to do more for Your Kingdom. May I to look to You for guidance when suffering comes.

Day 14

And the things you have heard me say in the presence of many witnesses entrust to reliable men who will also be qualified to teach others. Endure hardship with us like a good soldier of Christ Jesus. —2 TIMOTHY 2:2–3, NIV

We Are Honored

On Feb. 11, 1973, then-Captain Jeremiah Denton returned home after years of captivity as a prisoner of war in North Vietnam. He made his way down the steps of the plane, stopped in front of a microphone and said, "We are honored to have had the opportunity to serve our country under difficult circumstances."

I wonder if this is how the believer will feel when he stands one day before God? God entrusts to some of His servants—without explanation—the most difficult circumstances. Just look at Job, Joseph, Daniel and the early martyrs.

A young man released from an oppressive, atheistic regime was asked, "What was it like, being persecuted for your faith?"

"We thought it was the normal Christian life," was the

surprising, yet candid, reply.

He was right. It is Christians in the West who are living abnormally. Personally, I am grateful for the "abnormality." But if it doesn't last, we must not question, complain or become bitter. Instead let us accept each day as the Lord sends it, living obediently and faithfully and not fearing what may come. We know that the glory ahead will obliterate the grim past.

Prayer for the Day:

I want to be Your obedient servant, God. Please give me strength to do all that You ask, no matter how difficult. I will remember that no matter the trials, You will always be with me.

Day 15

I have brought you glory on earth by completing the work you gave me to do. —JOHN 17:4, NIV

It Is Enough!

Someone pointed out that Jesus did not feed all the hungry, heal all the sick or raise all the dead. Yet when He came to the end of His life's work just before His crucifixion, Jesus said, "I have finished the work which thou gavest me to do" (John 17:4, KJV). Hours later, His final words on the cross were "It is finished" (cf. John 19:30).

Often when I am exhausted, I have said, "It is enough!" We each have a limit, like the Plimsoll mark, a line around ocean tankers that indicates when a ship has reached capacity. He who made us knows just how much we can take. He never overloads us. But neither has He promised us strength for tasks that we take on without His direction.

I want God to so order my life that when the end comes, I can say, "I have finished the work which Thou gavest me to do."

I do not want to feel compelled to say "It is enough!" before I can say, with His help, "It is finished."

~

Prayer for the Day:

Sometimes, Lord, I let myself get overwhelmed with unnecessary tasks. Starting today, I will allow You to arrange and order my life so that I may accomplish Your will on earth.

Day 16

Our citizenship is in heaven. And we eagerly await a Savior from there, the Lord Jesus Christ, who, by the power that enables him to bring everything under his control, will transform our lowly bodies so that they will be like his glorious body. —PHILIPPIANS 3:20–21, NIV

Earth Is Not Our Home

In Psalm 37:35, David marvels at the wicked *"spreading himself like a green bay tree"* (KJV). Young's Literal Translation puts it: *"as a green native plant."*

We have a schefflera plant, or umbrella tree, in our living room. Because it is not native to where we live, it makes a nice houseplant, growing to 10 feet tall at most. But in a tropical climate such as Florida or Australia, it can grow to 40 feet.

Why should we wonder, then, when we Christians struggle? We are not native plants. The earth is not our home, and we can expect to have rough times. Our Lord promised us that. But we also have this promise: *"Blessed is the man who perseveres under trial, because* when he has stood the test, he will receive the crown of life that God has promised to those who love him" (James 1:12, NIV).

━━━∽

Prayer for the Day:

Lord, I look forward to the day when I will truly be at home—with You in heaven. As I look to that day, help me to be a faithful witness to Christ.

Day 17

Give, and it will be given to you. A good measure, pressed down,
shaken together and running over, will be poured into your lap.
For with the measure you use, it will be measured to you.
—Luke 6:38, NIV

Giving Timeless Gifts

One night some troublemakers broke into a
department store. They didn't steal or destroy
anything, but they had a wonderful time switching
price tags!

The next morning customers were puzzled and delighted to find
fur coats selling for $5, cold cream for $150, umbrellas for $1,000
and diamond rings for $2.

Has something come into your life that has switched price tags
on your values? Are things of time more valuable than things of
eternity? Are material gifts worth more than gifts of the Spirit? If
so, let me suggest some ways to re-establish your priorities and to
give some gifts that are timeless.

To your neighbors, nice or not, give thoughtful consideration. Be
slow to gossip, quick to sympathize, ready to help—praying all the

while that God will give them the necessary patience to live next to you.

To your parents, give loving appreciation for the years of time, effort and money that they invested in you. Do for them the little things that give them pleasure.

To your spouse, give a frank, honest reappraisal of yourself. Remember how much he or she has had to put up with and for how long. Ask yourself, "If I were my spouse, am I the sort of person I would want to come home to?"

To your children, although you are not a perfect parent, you can give them more of the one they have—and make that one more loving. Be available, knowing that a parent needs to be, as God is, *"a very present help in trouble"* (Psalm 46:1, KJV). Give your children the eternal verities of the Word of God.

These are gifts of the heart and of the spirit. There are those you love who long for (and desperately need) these gifts. Commit yourself to give them those gifts timeless and eternal.

~~➤~~

Prayer for the Day:

Forgive me, Lord, for paying more attention to my needs than to the needs of those whom You have called me to serve. Please give me strength to serve others—and You—with joy.

Day 18

Our gospel came to you not simply with words, but also with power, with the Holy Spirit and with deep conviction. You know how we lived among you for your sake. You became imitators of us and of the Lord; in spite of severe suffering, you welcomed the message with the joy given by the Holy Spirit.
—1 THESSALONIANS 1:5–6, NIV

Parents Are Not Miracle Workers

As parents, we may be tempted to try to do God's work and to neglect the very responsibilities that He has given to us. He asks us to take care of the possible and to trust Him for the impossible.

How often we have tried to convict our loved ones of their sin and their need of the Savior, to make them want God, to make them read their Bibles and to pray and to live for Him.

But our responsibility is to minister lovingly to the immediate needs of our families, whether it is by providing a happy home, by preparing a good meal and washing clothes or by offering words of encouragement, love and appreciation.

And our responsibility is to pray.

God will do His part. Salvation and love for God, the willingness to come under His authority, and the longing to do His will joyfully are miracles of grace. And miracles are in God's department, not ours.

—◆—

Prayer for the Day:

Father, I confess that I have tried in my own strength to bring my loved ones into a relationship with Christ. I relinquish them to the conviction of the Holy Spirit, and I ask You to guide me as I live out the Gospel among them.

Day 19

The Strongest Love

To save us from eternal death, God had to give the very
life of His Son, Jesus.

God would send His Son to earth as a human baby
too weak to lift up His own head. He would learn how
to crawl, how to stand, how to run.

When He had grown to manhood, He would bring men back to
the God whom they had forgotten. He would tell them: "The Lord
our God loves you" (cf. John 3:16), "You must love Him with all
your heart and soul and mind and strength" (cf. Matthew 22:37),
and "You must love others as much as you love yourself"
(cf. Matthew 22:39).

Then He would show them, as well as tell them, what God meant
by "love" when He fed the hungry, healed the sick and made the

blind to see.

Finally, He would show them the greatest love of all: He would die for them so that the way to God would be opened.

After that, no matter how far a person wandered, no matter how big the sin, there would still be this way back to God. For love like this would be stronger than sin—stronger than death itself.

$$\sim$$

Prayer for the Day:

Thank you, Lord, for sending Jesus Christ to die for my sins. I will tell others of His great sacrifice so that they may find new life through Him.

Day 20

There is now no condemnation for those who are in Christ Jesus, because through Christ Jesus the law of the Spirit of life set me free from the law of sin and death. —ROMANS 8:1–2, NIV

"Remember Your Position"

The local sheriff had tightened the requirements for his deputies. They had to qualify on the firing range, where the distance had been extended by 10 yards. Each deputy had 18 seconds to get off 12 shots.

The deputy with the best shot was a personal friend of ours named George. But the day before the trials, he had been fitted with trifocals. When his turn came, he drew a bead on the target.

"Suddenly," he told me later, "I began to perspire. And when I perspire, my glasses fog up. There I was with a bead drawn on the target, and all I could see was fog."

But then he remembered what he'd been taught in the Navy: "If you ever lose sight of the target, just remember your position."

So with time running out, George just held his position and

pulled the trigger as fast as he could. When he took off his glasses and wiped them, he saw that every shot had hit the bull's-eye.

There are times as Christians when we, for some reason, lose sight of our target, which is to glorify the Lord. Tears blur our vision. Unexplained tragedy raises questions that cannot be answered and shakes our faith to its foundations.

Then we must remember that our position is "in Christ." As if we are tired or hurt children, He will gather both us and our loads.

Though we may not see the target, if we just "remember our position," we won't miss.

Prayer for the Day:

I know that I am Your child, Father, and You will allow nothing to separate me from Your love, which is in Christ. Remind me of my position when life threatens my trust in You.

"Come, you who are blessed by my Father; take your inheritance. ... For I was hungry and you gave me something to eat, I was thirsty and you gave me something to drink, I was a stranger and you invited me in, I needed clothes and you clothed me, I was sick and you looked after me, I was in prison and you came to visit me." —MATTHEW 25:34–36, NIV

What the Left Hand Is Doing

"He doesn't want his right hand to know that his left hand is doing nothing," a friend said of a stingy relative, wryly reversing Jesus' advice to not let the left hand know what the right is doing.

Those who have affected my life most deeply for good have seldom, if ever, been aware of the fact. On the other hand, people who think themselves a blessing seldom are.

Jesus told us in Matthew 25 that at the final judgment, He will separate the people one from another, as a shepherd would divide sheep and goats, sending the sheep to the right and the goats to the left.

"*Come, you who are blessed by my Father; take your inheritance,*" He will say to the sheep. "*For I was hungry and you gave me something to eat, ... I was a stranger and you invited me in, ... I was sick and you looked after me, I was in prison and you came to visit me*" (Matthew 25:34–36, NIV).

But to the goats He will say the opposite, commanding, "*Depart from me, you who are cursed, into the eternal fire prepared for the devil and his angels*" (Matthew 25:41, NIV). The goats will have ignored His every need, which, He explained, are the needs of the least of His brethren.

Those who minister to His needs are as unaware of their goodness and kindness as those who are indifferent are unaware of their indifference. Perhaps this is why Jesus warned against giving alms before men. And not letting your right hand know what the left is doing.

❧

Prayer for the Day:

God, please help me to do everything with the attitude that I am doing it for Christ and in His Name. I want to be His hands and feet to a world in need.

Day 22

This is what the Lord says, he who made the earth, the Lord who formed it and established it—the Lord is his name: "Call to me and I will answer you and tell you great and unsearchable things you do not know." —JEREMIAH 33:2–3, NIV

No Answering Service

I desperately needed to make some travel arrangements. I called an airline and heard a man's recorded voice intone, "Due to heavy traffic, we are unable to help you at this time. If you will kindly wait, someone will be with you shortly."

I tried a second airline. After listening to repeated ringing, I heard a female voice say, "Thank you for calling. Due to the increase in calls, there will be a slight delay in answering. To assist us in answering your question …"

I turned to a third airline only to receive the same noncommittal answering service.

So, I started all over. Each time I got the same response. One time I dialed the wrong number, and who do you suppose answered? You guessed it: an answering service.

Frustrated, I tried to call my husband, who happened to be in Nova Scotia. I instead reached one of his associates who, while not being as satisfactory as my husband, was certainly better than an answering service. He put me in touch with a local travel agent, and my problem eventually was solved.

How grateful we can be that God has no answering service! In fact, He says: *"It shall come to pass, that before they call, I will answer; and while they are yet speaking, I will hear"* (Isaiah 65:24, KJV).

~

Prayer for the Day:

You are always attentive to my prayers, Lord. Please give me a spirit that listens for Your answer and responds in faith.

Day 23

Precious in the sight of the Lord is the death of his saints.
—PSALM 116:15, NIV

Coming Home

"I shall miss Mother this Christmas," the clerk in the local store told me. Her mother had died recently, and this would be the first Christmas without her.

When her mother entered the hospital, the doctor told the family to stay out of the room so that she could rest.

"So I stayed out in the hall," the clerk recalled. "Finally, I could stand it no longer, and I went in. Mother said, 'I thought you'd never come!'"

Blinking back tears, the clerk added with a smile, "I think those will be the first words she'll say to me when I get to heaven."

Psalm 116:15 says, *"Precious in the sight of the Lord is the death of his saints"* (KJV). I didn't understand this verse until I realized that I had been looking at death from my perspective, not from God's point of view.

Ever since my children left home for school or to get married, their return has brought a joy that one understands only when their children grow up, leave home and then return. Just as *"there is joy in the presence of the angels of God over one sinner that repenteth"* (Luke 15:10, KJV), so, too, there is joy in heaven as each child of God comes home.

⤙⟶

Prayer for the Day:

Lord, death is painful because it separates me from loved ones. When death invades my life, remind me that You are in heaven, eagerly awaiting the arrival of all who have put their faith in Jesus.

Day 24

Each of us will give an account of himself to God. Therefore let us stop passing judgment on one another. Instead, make up your mind not to put any stumbling block or obstacle in your brother's way. —ROMANS 14:12–13, NIV

Forgery?

"I don't trust her," an older Christian said of a newcomer to the household of God. "She's a phony."

Strange, I thought to myself. Wouldn't the Father rather we welcome a phony than put down a genuine new believer, however odd or difficult that new believer might appear to be?

A former director of the Metropolitan Museum of Art in New York City is reputed to have said, "Although it is a mistake to collect a fake, an error every adventurous connoisseur has made, it is an absolute sin to brand as a forgery an authentic work of art."

Objects of art are complete and static. But Christians, I hope, are growing, even though in some that growth may be imperceptible. However, Paul has given us the simplest common denominator in 1 Corinthians 12:3: *"No one can say, 'Jesus is Lord'* except by the Holy Spirit" (RSV). Perhaps the Father watches how we welcome those who pass Paul's test—even though we might distrust them or might not like them because for some reason they fail to pass our own standards. But wouldn't we rather welcome a fake than brand as forgery an authentic work of grace?

Prayer for the Day:

God, I confess that I have often judged other people and held them to a standard I myself have not met. Please forgive me and replace my judgmental attitude with Your love for them.

Day 25

Mistakes

Some fishermen in the highlands of Scotland came into a little Scottish inn late one afternoon for a cup of tea. As one was describing "the one that got away" to his friends, he flung out his hands in the typical fisherman's gesture. He did so just as the waitress was setting down his cup of tea. The resulting collision left a huge tea stain spreading on the whitewashed wall. The fisherman apologized profusely.

Another man seated nearby said, "Never mind." Rising, he took a crayon from his pocket and began to sketch around the ugly, brown stain. Slowly there emerged the head of a magnificent royal stag with large antlers. The man was Edwin Landseer, England's foremost painter of animals.

Now if an artist can do that with an ugly, brown stain, what can God do with my sins and mistakes if I but give them to Him?

———

Prayer for the Day:

If not for Your mercy, Lord, my sin would overwhelm me and separate me from You. I am amazed at how You have turned my broken life into something You can use for Your glory.

Day 26

Your word is a lamp to my feet and a light for my path. I have taken an oath and confirmed it, that I will follow your righteous laws. —PSALM 119:105–106, NIV

The Reference Point

The Pennsylvania State Highway Department once set out to build a bridge, working from both sides. When the two crews of workers reached the middle of the waterway, they were 13 feet to one side of each other. Alfred Steinberg, writing some time ago in the *Saturday Evening Post*, went on to explain that each crew had used its own reference point.

A small bronze disk at Meades Ranch Triangulation Station in Osborne, Kan., marks the place where the 39th parallel crosses the 98th meridian. The National Geodetic Survey, a federal agency whose business it is to locate the exact position of every point in the United States, used this scientifically recognized reference point until the advent of an even more precise reference system, the global positioning system (GPS). All ocean liners and commercial planes rely on the Survey. The government can build no dams nor can it shoot off a missile without this agency to tell it exact locations—to the very inch.

The reference point (or GPS) for the Christian is the Bible. All values, judgments and attitudes must be gauged in relationship to this reference point.

"Location by approximation," Steinberg's article goes on to say, "can be costly and dangerous."

Prayer for the Day:

Help me, Father, to base all of my decisions on the truth of Your Word, the Bible. As I read it, help me to understand it and put its commands into practice.

Day 27

All the believers were one in heart and mind. No one claimed that any of his possessions was his own, but they shared everything they had. With great power the apostles continued to testify to the resurrection of the Lord Jesus, and much grace was upon them all. —ACTS 4:32–33, NIV

The Coat

ne semester at Wheaton College, a friend and I decided to give up the privilege of eating in the upper dining hall and move to the lower dining hall in order to give the difference in cost to a student we knew on campus who was in real need.

The upper dining hall was cafeteria-style. Students ate at small tables and the atmosphere was decidedly more pleasant. The lower dining hall was in the basement of Williston Hall, a girls' dormitory, and students ate family-style at long tables. The difference per semester wasn't all that much. But there was a need, and we felt this was an opportunity to help.

Later I saw the student who was in need wearing a coat that

I couldn't afford. My instant reaction was indignation. Then it was as if the Lord Himself asked, "Are you doing this for her—or for Me?"

I had to admit that we were doing it because we loved Him.

"That's all I wanted to know," He said.

It was all I needed to know. After that, she could have worn sable and it would have made no difference to me.

———✦———

Prayer for the Day:

Lord, You have blessed me and met my needs. Help me to be as generous to others and remember to do all things for the glory of Your Name.

Day 28

Waiting

ur son Ned had reached the point in life when he wanted a bicycle more than anything. He had been playing with his friend Joel that fall and wanted one just like Joel's—today!

"No," Bill said. "Wait until Christmas."

And that was that.

So Joel lent Ned his new bike for a week. Before the week was over, Ned knew that Joel's bike would be too small for him in a few months. So he decided he needed a larger model.

The next week he saw one advertised with the works: three speeds, spring suspension, butterfly handles, triple brakes, slicks. This was the one he had to have, and it was still two months until Christmas!

Then I understood, as never before, why God does not answer all of our prayers right away. Today we may be beseeching Him for things that we would not want six months from now.

However, most of our prayers are not "bicycle prayers."

When we pray according to God's will (that the prodigal will return; that the sorrowing may find His comfort; that He will work each situation out for our good and His glory), we know that He hears us, for each of these requests is what He wants.

But at times He has us wait for the answers.

The Psalm 27 command *"Wait on the Lord"* (v. 14, KJV) reads in the old Book of Common Prayer: "O tarry thou the Lord's leisure."

And to many of us impatient souls, how "leisurely" He seems at times!

———✦———

Prayer for the Day:

God, thank You for listening to my prayers and answering them in Your time, not mine. When Your answers are not what I want, I will be patient and wait on You.

Day 29

Encourage the young men to be self-controlled. In everything set them an example by doing what is good. In your teaching show integrity, seriousness and soundness of speech that cannot be condemned, so that those who oppose you may be ashamed because they have nothing bad to say about us.
—Titus 2:6–8, NIV

Tipping the Scales

ver the years many people had an influence on our children. My parents; our pastor, Calvin Thielman; and several of Bill's associates were among them. But not everyone was an inspiration.

At one conference, one of our sons watched a difficult Christian leader repeatedly rebuke, correct and embarrass an older Christian who happened to be working under him.

Someone once said: "No person is absolutely unnecessary. They can always serve as a horrible example."

Day after day, our son quietly watched and listened, unable to intervene.

Not once did the older man show anything but Christian graciousness and humility. Never once did he get angry and complain. Not once did he strike back. He was a perfect illustration of J.B. Rotherham's translation of Proverbs 24:25: *"To reprovers, one should be pleasant."**

Neither the horrible example nor the gentle saint was aware he was being observed. Neither knew that the scales in one young heart were being tilted inevitably toward the Savior because of an older man's close resemblance to Him when under attack.

⌐━━━

Prayer for the Day:

God, help me live as Your faithful disciple, exhibiting patience, grace and humility in my speech and actions. May my life point others toward Jesus Christ.

*From the *Emphasized Bible* by J.B. Rotherham

Day 30

Do not be anxious about anything, but in everything, by prayer and petition, with thanksgiving, present your requests to God. And the peace of God, which transcends all understanding, will guard your hearts and your minds in Christ Jesus.
—Philippians 4:6–7, NIV

"With Thanksgiving"

L ike an electric shock, the name of someone I loved dearly flashed into my mind at 3 a.m. and jolted me awake. So I lay there praying for the one who was trying hard to run away from God. When it is dark and the imagination runs wild, there are fears that only a mother can understand.

Suddenly the Lord said to me, "Quit studying the problems and start studying the promises."

So I turned on the light and got out my Bible. The first passage that came to me was Philippians 4:6–7, *"Be anxious for nothing, but in everything by prayer and supplication, with thanksgiving, let your requests be made known to God; and the peace of God, which surpasses all understanding, will guard your hearts and minds through Christ*

Jesus" (NKJV). Suddenly I realized the missing ingredient in my prayers had been "with thanksgiving." So I put down my Bible and spent time worshiping God for who He is and what He is. Even contemplating what little we do comprehend of God dissolves doubts, reinforces faith and restores joy. I began to thank God for giving me this loved one in the first place. I even thanked Him for the difficult spots that taught me so much.

Do you know what happened? It was as if suddenly someone turned on the lights in my mind and heart, and the little fears and worries, which like mice and cockroaches had been nibbling away in the darkness, suddenly scuttled for cover.

That was when I learned that worship and worry cannot live in the same heart; they are mutually exclusive.

―――✦―――

Prayer for the Day:

How reassuring that I can cast all of my worries into Your steady hands, Lord. Forgive me for the times that I have forgotten to offer You praise and worship when I make my requests.

Day 31

Who shall separate us from the love of Christ? Shall trouble or hardship or persecution or famine or nakedness or danger or sword? ... No, in all these things we are more than conquerors through him who loved us. —ROMANS 8:35, 37, NIV

"Why Me?"

Malcolm Muggeridge, the British journalist and author, was to speak at All Souls Church in London. He answered questions in an after-service coffee, mostly defending his conversion to Christianity. When the pastor sensed time was up, he called for one more question. After dealing with that question, Muggeridge noticed a small boy in a wheelchair trying to say something. He stopped. "There is someone who wants to ask me a question. I will wait and answer it," he said.

Again the boy struggled to get the words out, but nothing came.

"Take your time," said Muggeridge reassuringly. "I want to hear what you have to ask, and I'll not leave until I hear it."

Finally, after a struggle that produced only agonized contortions, the boy blurted out, "You say there is a God who loves us."

Muggeridge agreed.

"Then—why me?"

Silence filled the room. The boy was silent. The audience was silent. Muggeridge was silent. Finally, he asked, "If you were fit, would you have come to hear me tonight?"

The boy shook his head.

Again Muggeridge was silent. Then, "God has asked a hard thing of you," he said. "But remember He asked something even harder of Jesus Christ. He died for you. Maybe this was His way of making sure you'd hear of His love and come to put your faith in Him."

❧

Prayer for the Day:

Father, thank You for Your sovereign care. I praise You for working all things in my life for Your glory and my good. Help me to see the light of Your love when my path is painfully dark.

Steps to Peace With God

STEP 1   God's Purpose: Peace and Life

God loves you and wants you to experience peace and life—abundant and eternal.

THE BIBLE SAYS ...

"We have peace with God through our Lord Jesus Christ."
Romans 5:1, NIV

Since God planned for us to have peace and the abundant life right now, why are most people not having this experience?

"For God so loved the world that He gave His only begotten Son, that whoever believes in Him should not perish but have everlasting life."
John 3:16, NKJV

"I have come that they may have life, and that they may have it more abundantly." *John 10:10, NKJV*

STEP 2 Our Problem: Separation

God created us in His own image to have an abundant life. He did not make us as robots to automatically love and obey Him, but gave us a will and a freedom of choice.

We chose to disobey God and go our own willful way. We still make this choice today. This results in separation from God.

THE BIBLE SAYS ...

"For all have sinned and fall short of the glory of God." *Romans 3:23, NIV*

"For the wages of sin is death, but the gift of God is eternal life in Christ Jesus our Lord." *Romans 6:23, NIV*

Our choice results in separation from God.

People (Sinful)

God (Holy)

Our Attempts

Through the ages, individuals have tried in many ways to bridge this gap ... without success ...

THE BIBLE SAYS ...

"There is a way that seems right to a man, but in the end it leads to death." *Proverbs 14:12, NIV*

"But your iniquities have separated you from your God; and your sins have hidden His face from you, so that He will not hear." *Isaiah 59:2, NKJV*

There is only one remedy for this problem of separation.

STEP 3   God's Remedy: The Cross

Jesus Christ is the only answer to this problem. He died on the cross and rose from the grave, paying the penalty for our sin and bridging the gap between God and people.

THE BIBLE SAYS ...

"For there is one God and one mediator between God and men, the man Christ Jesus." *1 Timothy 2:5, NIV*

"For Christ also suffered once for sins, the just for the unjust, that He might bring us to God." *1 Peter 3:18, NKJV*

"But God demonstrates his own love for us in this: While we were still sinners, Christ died for us." *Romans 5:8, NIV*

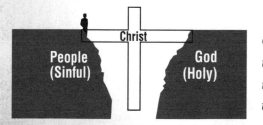

God has provided the only way ... we must make the choice ...

STEP 4 Our Response: Receive Christ

We must trust Jesus Christ and receive Him by personal invitation ...

THE BIBLE SAYS ...

"Behold, I stand at the door and knock. If anyone hears My voice and opens the door, I will come in to him and dine with him, and he with Me." *Revelation 3:20, NKJV*

"But as many as received Him, to them He gave the right to become children of God, to those who believe in His name." *John 1:12, NKJV*

"If you confess with your mouth the Lord Jesus and believe in your heart that God has raised Him from the dead, you will be saved." *Romans 10:9, NKJV*

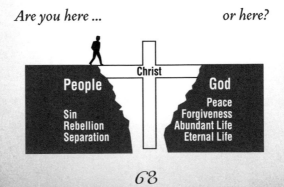

68

Is there any good reason why you cannot receive Jesus Christ right now?

How to receive Christ:

1. Admit your need (I am a sinner).
2. Be willing to turn from your sins (repent).
3. Believe that Jesus Christ died for you on the cross and rose from the grave.
4. Through prayer, invite Jesus Christ to come in and control your life through the Holy Spirit. (Receive Him as Lord and Savior.)

What to Pray:

Dear Lord Jesus,

I know that I am a sinner, and I ask for Your forgiveness. I believe You died for my sins and rose from the dead. I turn from my sins and invite You to come into my heart and life. I want to trust and follow You as my Lord and Savior.

In Your Name, Amen.

_____   _____
Date   Signature

God's Assurance: His Word

If you prayed this prayer,

THE BIBLE SAYS ...

"For 'whoever calls on the name of the Lord shall be saved.'" *Romans 10:13, NKJV*

Did you sincerely ask Jesus Christ to come into your life? Where is He right now? What has He given you?

"For it is by grace you have been saved, through faith—and this not from yourselves, it is the gift of God—not by works, so that no one can boast." *Ephesians 2:8–9, NIV*

The Bible Says ...

"He who has the Son has life; he who does not have the Son of God does not have life. These things I have written to you who believe in the name of the Son of God, that you may know that you have eternal life, and that you may continue to believe in the name of the Son of God." *1 John 5:12–13, NKJV*

Receiving Christ, we are born into God's family through the supernatural work of the Holy Spirit who indwells every believer. This is called regeneration or the "new birth."

This is just the beginning of a wonderful new life in Christ. To deepen this relationship, you should:
1. Read your Bible every day to know Christ better.
2. Talk to God in prayer every day.
3. Tell others about Christ.
4. Worship, fellowship, and serve with other Christians in a church where Christ is preached.
5. As Christ's representative in a needy world, demonstrate your new life by your love and concern for others.

> God bless you as you do.
> Billy Graham

If you are committing your life to Christ, please let us know!

We would like to send you Bible study materials to help you grow in your faith.

The Billy Graham Evangelistic Association exists to support and extend the evangelistic calling and ministries of Billy Graham and Franklin Graham by proclaiming the Gospel of the Lord Jesus Christ to all we can by every effective means available to us and by equipping others to do the same.

Our desire is to introduce as many people as we can to the person of Jesus Christ, so that they might experience His love and forgiveness.

Your prayers are the most important way to support us in this ministry. We are grateful for the dedicated prayer support we receive. We are also grateful for those who support us with financial contributions.

Billy Graham Evangelistic Association
1 Billy Graham Parkway
Charlotte, North Carolina 28201-0001
billygraham.org
Toll-free: 1-877-2GRAHAM
(1-877-247-2426)

Billy Graham Evangelistic Association of Canada
20 Hopewell Way NE
Calgary, Alberta T3J 5H5
billygraham.ca
Toll-free: 1-888-393-0003